Short Stack Editions | Volume 16

Peaches

by Beth Lipton

Short Stack Editions

Publisher: Nick Fauchald
Creative Director: Rotem Raffe
Editor: Kaitlyn Goalen
Copy Editor: Abby Tannenbaum
Director of Development: Mackenzie Smith

ISBN 978-0-9907853-5-4

Printed in New York City
July 2015

Table of Contents

Desserts

Sauce

Drinks

We've always thought of peaches as a bit brazen, and, if we're being honest, one-dimensional.

The fuzzy skin, the slap-in-the-face sweetness, the unruly juiciness—a peach demands the spotlight of summer desserts, and leaves nothing to the imagination.

Or so we thought.

Then we dug into the recipes of Beth Lipton, for whom peaches are something far more complex. She addresses the Golden Retriever-esque likability of the fruit, acknowledging it for its sweet nature. But then she demands more of the peach than the usual popularity contest, making it rise to a spectrum of challenges as wide as a piquant Bloody Mary, a rich rack of lamb and a delicate ceviche. She dares peaches to reveal their complexity.

Through Beth's recipes, peaches have evolved for us. We've come to think about their acidity, their creamy enriching texture, even their slightly ferment-y funk just as much as their sugar.

This newfound perspective has made our summer cooking repertoire even sweeter. We hope it does the same for you.

—The Editors

Introduction

The farmers' markets of my childhood on Long Island weren't glamorous and fashionable like they are today. They were dusty roadside places to stop off for cheap produce on the way home from a long day at the beach, not destinations where chefs and celebrities shopped. For a tired kid in a damp, sandy swimsuit, a trip to the farmers' market was a real eye-roller. But there was a reward for patience. If I didn't fidget or fight with my big brother while my mother bought corn and tomatoes for dinner, I got a big, soft, fragrant peach, warm from the sun, bursting with sweetness. I would shuffle around the market, sniffing the flowers, eyeing the jams and pies on display, avoiding the bees—all the while greedily sinking my teeth into the peach's juicy flesh and letting my fingers get all sticky as I nibbled every last bit off the stone.

Peaches are synonymous with sweetness and goodness. How are you? "Peachy." Or, "Everything's peaches and cream." No wonder: There is so much to love about a peach. That odd, endearingly fuzzy exterior, which at the peak of ripeness gives off an intoxicatingly, uniquely *peachy* scent; the sunny yellow (or creamy white) flesh, with its pretty splash of pink close to the stone; the sweetness, almost indecently so, just on the edge of being too much. You can't eat a peach absently or elegantly. Even if you try to be civilized about it and cut the peach into pieces beforehand, it'll still drip all over your hands and chin. You have to pay attention. It's as if the notion of mindful eating was created just for peaches.

And if eating peaches out of hand is a sensual experience, cooking and baking with them is pure fun. They're sweet, sure, but their merits extend far beyond sugar content. There is a complexity and subtlety hiding behind that sweetness: a touch of acid, a creaminess that can create beautiful viscosity when blended or pureed. They love to hang with chiles, tomatoes and cucumbers, and they have more flexibility than you may think. Want to toss them into a salad? Whir them in a blender for a cocktail? Cook them into a tangy barbecue sauce? Bake them into muffins or a pie? Go for it. Peaches can do it all. Like an ideal party guest, they show up looking pretty, get along with everybody and leave you feeling happy they were there and wistful when they're gone.

These days, a farmers' market trip is more of an event than it was when I was a kid now that they're so trendy and sexy. Luckily, I no longer have to behave to get a peach. But it still feels like a reward—for what, I don't know—to bite into a fresh, sun-warmed summer peach.

—*Beth Lipton*

Recipes

Peach Best Practices

Free vs. cling

There are thousands of varieties of peaches, but the two main types are freestone and clingstone. When you open a freestone peach, the pit separates easily from the flesh. With a clingstone peach, the stone sticks to the flesh, so it's harder to remove. Unfortunately, you can't tell which it is just by looking at a peach; you need to know the variety. The types can be used interchangeably in recipes, but freestones are easier to manage, especially if you're pitting several at a time. If you find yourself with clingstone peaches and need to pit them, here's how to make the task easier: Cut the peach in half horizontally. Twist the peach gently, which will release the flesh from half of the peach. Cut the other half, where the pit is still attached, in half again, this time going the other way, and twist again; now you have another quarter loosened from the pit. Finally, cut or pull the pit away from the remaining flesh.

Yellow vs. white

Both freestone and clingstone peaches come in varieties with yellow and white flesh. The more common yellow-fleshed peaches are more acidic, while the white ones are more delicate and purely sweet. They are interchangeable, though the yellow ones will impart a slightly stronger peach flavor, making them preferable for recipes in which peaches are paired with other strong flavors.

What's up with the flat ones?

Donut or Saturn peaches, the squat ones you often find at farmers' markets, are a genetic mutation. Like other peaches, they come yellow- or white-fleshed, and may be clingstone or freestone. They aren't as easy to use for cooking, as they're smaller and harder to prepare, but they're just as delicious as regular peaches for eating out of hand.

How to pick a peach

Scent. Peaches are part of the rose family, which is why their fragrance is so heady. Pick one up and give it a whiff; it should smell sweet and undeniably peachy.

Appearance. The color, whether it's pure yellow or blushy pink, indicates the variety, not the ripeness. You want a peach that's vibrant in color, no matter what its hue. Avoid peaches with a greenish color: they were probably picked too early and won't get very sweet. Also, check the peach for bruises. If you can get a deal on lightly bruised peaches, buy them— it won't matter if you're using them in preserves or gazpacho.

Texture. You want a peach that's soft, but not mushy. Buy some that are a bit firmer than others so you'll be able to eat or cook with them over a few days. Don't squeeze too hard when feeling them; they bruise easily. Just give them a light press on the shoulder, near the stem.

Storing your peaches

Keep them on the counter, ideally in a single layer, stem-side down. If they get very soft, refrigerate them for a day or two (or just eat them already—what are you waiting for?).

There's more than one way to skin a peach

The traditional way to peel peaches is to cut an X at the bottom with a paring knife, drop them into a pot of boiling water for 20 to 30 seconds, then plunge them into an ice bath. The skins will slip off easily. But if you're lazy like me, there's an easier way: Invest $5 in a serrated peeler. This little miracle gadget lets you peel delicate fruit like peaches and tomatoes without losing the flesh or boiling water.

Breakfast Cobbler

I love making fruit desserts—especially rustic, unfussy ones like crisps and cobblers—any time of year, but particularly in the summer. And I almost always include peaches, whether they stand alone or comingle with berries. Inevitably, I end up eating the leftovers for breakfast (cold, usually while standing in front of the open fridge). So I figured, why not cut the sugar a bit, use whole-grain flour and just call it breakfast in the first place?

1¾ pounds peaches (6 to 7 medium)—peeled, pitted and sliced (about 4 cups)

½ cup granulated sugar

1 tablespoon lemon juice

Kosher salt

8 tablespoons (1 stick) unsalted butter, melted

1 cup white whole-wheat flour (*see Note*)

½ cup packed dark brown sugar

1 teaspoon baking powder

¼ teaspoon baking soda

1 teaspoon cinnamon

¼ cup sour cream

¾ cup whole milk

2 teaspoons cornstarch

Plain or vanilla yogurt for serving, optional

serves
8

In a large bowl, stir together the peaches, granulated sugar, lemon juice and a pinch of salt. Let stand at room temperature while you prepare the remaining cobbler ingredients.

Preheat the oven to 375°. Spread the melted butter in a 9-by-13-inch baking dish (preferably glass). In a bowl, whisk together the flour, brown sugar, baking powder, baking soda, cinnamon and ⅛ teaspoon of salt, breaking up any lumps of brown sugar. In a separate small bowl, whisk the sour cream and milk together, then add to the dry ingredients and stir until just combined (do not overmix). Pour the batter over the butter in the baking dish as evenly as possible; do not stir.

Stir the cornstarch into the peach mixture. Pour the peach mixture evenly over the batter in the baking dish; do not stir. Bake for 40 to 45 minutes or until golden brown. Serve warm with yogurt on the side, if desired.

Note: White whole-wheat flour is made from a type of wheat that is lighter in both color and texture than typical whole-wheat flour. It's readily available in supermarkets. But if you already have both all-purpose and regular whole-wheat flour on hand, you can use ½ cup of each in this recipe.

Whole-Grain Peach Pancakes with Raspberry Sauce

The great Auguste Escoffier created Peach Melba in the late 1800s to honor opera singer Nellie Melba. At my house, things aren't quite so fancy pants; you'll find me flipping pancakes in my pajamas on a Sunday, more likely listening to Gomez than Verdi. But I raise my half-empty coffee mug to the great chef for his ingenious pairing of sweet, creamy peaches with tart raspberries via these crowd-pleasing flapjacks.

For the raspberry sauce:

4 cups raspberries, divided

1 to 2 tablespoons fresh orange juice

1 to 3 tablespoons honey

Pinch of salt

For the pancakes:

1 cup white whole-wheat flour (*see Note*)

½ cup old-fashioned or quick-cooking oats (not instant)

1½ teaspoons baking powder

¼ teaspoon baking soda

¾ teaspoon salt

3 large eggs

¾ cup sour cream or plain yogurt (preferably full fat)

¼ cup whole milk

3 tablespoons pure maple syrup, plus more for serving

1 teaspoon vanilla extract

1 tablespoon melted unsalted butter or coconut oil, plus more for the griddle

2 small peaches (8 to 10 ounces) —peeled, pitted and thinly sliced

Additional butter, for serving

serves 4

Make the sauce: Blend 2 cups of raspberries in a food processor, then push them through a fine-mesh sieve into a bowl. Add the remaining berries, 1 tablespoon of orange juice, 1 tablespoon of honey and salt and

mix with a fork, mashing the berries. Taste and add more juice and/or honey, if desired. Cover and refrigerate until ready to serve.

Make the pancakes: Preheat the oven to 200°. In a large bowl, whisk together the flour, oats, baking powder, baking soda and salt. In a blender, combine the eggs, yogurt, milk, maple syrup, vanilla and butter; blend just until smooth. Pour the yogurt mixture into the flour mixture and fold together just until combined (don't worry if you still see a few stray bits of unincorporated flour).

Preheat a griddle or large skillet over medium-low heat. Brush with butter (or coconut oil) and drop about 3 tablespoons of batter onto the griddle for each pancake, spreading each spoonful of batter into a circle with the back of your spoon. Place 2 or 3 peach slices on each pancake. Do not overcrowd the griddle. Cook until bubbles appear on the edges of the pancakes and the undersides are golden (lift up an edge gently with a spatula to check), about 2 minutes. Carefully flip the pancakes and cook until the other sides are golden and the pancakes are cooked through, 1 to 2 minutes longer. Transfer the pancakes to a platter and keep warm in the oven while you repeat with the remaining batter and peaches.

Serve the pancakes warm with additional butter and raspberry sauce on the side (and maple syrup as well, if you like).

Note: White whole-wheat flour is made from a type of wheat that is lighter in both color and texture than typical whole-wheat flour. It's readily available in supermarkets. But if you already have both all-purpose and regular whole-wheat flour on hand, you can use ½ cup of each in this recipe.

Spiced Peach Streusel Muffins

It's no secret that muffins are just an excuse to eat cupcakes for breakfast. I have no issue with that. In fact, I say if you're going to do it, go all the way: fill the muffins with luscious peaches and plenty of warm spices, then top them off with a buttery, brown sugary streusel. If anyone balks, tell them there are oats and heart-healthy pecans in there, too.

For the streusel:

½ cup packed dark brown sugar

¼ cup all-purpose flour

2 tablespoons old-fashioned oats

½ teaspoon cinnamon

Pinch of kosher salt

2 tablespoons unsalted butter, melted and cooled

¼ cup chopped pecans, toasted

For the muffins:

¾ cup old-fashioned oats

¼ cup oat bran

¾ cup whole-wheat flour

¾ cup all-purpose flour

⅔ cup packed dark brown sugar

2 teaspoons baking powder

2 teaspoons cinnamon

1 teaspoon ground ginger

¼ teaspoon freshly grated nutmeg

½ teaspoon salt

¼ teaspoon baking soda

¾ cup plain full-fat yogurt

½ cup whole milk

¼ cup maple syrup

1 large egg

1 teaspoon vanilla extract

8 tablespoons (1 stick) unsalted butter, melted and cooled

2 small peaches (8 to 10 ounces) —peeled, pitted and cut into ¼-inch pieces

makes 12 muffins

Preheat the oven to 400°. Line a 12-cup muffin tin with liners or grease with cooking spray.

Make the streusel: In a bowl, combine the brown sugar, flour, oats, cinnamon and salt; mix well. Stir in the butter until the mixture is evenly moistened and crumbly. Toss in the pecans. Refrigerate until ready to use.

Make the muffins: In a large bowl, combine the oats, oat bran, both flours, brown sugar, baking powder, spices, salt and baking soda; whisk until well mixed, breaking up any lumps of brown sugar. In a separate bowl, whisk together the yogurt, milk, maple syrup, egg, vanilla and melted butter. Pour the yogurt mixture into the flour mixture and stir until nearly combined, then fold in the peaches. Using a ¼-cup measuring cup or an ice cream scoop, divide the batter among the muffin cups. Sprinkle the streusel on top.

Bake for 20 minutes or until a toothpick inserted into the center of a muffin comes out clean. Place the muffin tin on a wire rack and let cool for 10 minutes, then release the muffins from the tin onto the rack and let cool before serving.

Tip: If you want to keep the streusel from getting all over your muffin tin, hold a round cookie cutter over each batter-filled cup as you sprinkle on the streusel.

Spicy Peach Gazpacho

Peaches and tomatoes, those two summer superstars, come together in this quintessential hot-weather soup. My husband, whose gazpacho is magical, swears by Knudsen Organic Very Veggie Juice as the base for his, as do I. This soup is best at the height of peach season, but you can make it in colder months by using a 10-ounce bag of frozen peaches (you don't even have to thaw them) and omitting the fresh peach garnish.

3 tablespoons extra-virgin olive oil, divided

⅓ small sweet onion (such as Vidalia), chopped (about ½ cup)

1 jalapeño, half or all seeds removed (see Note), chopped

Salt and freshly ground black pepper

1 large garlic clove, minced

1 pound tomatoes, preferably plum or Campari (about 6), chopped

½ cucumber—peeled, seeded and chopped

3 tablespoons white wine vinegar

2 tablespoons chopped fresh basil

4 small peaches (about 1 pound)—peeled, pitted and chopped, divided

½ to 1 cup vegetable juice (such as Knudsen Organic Very Veggie Juice)

1 to 2 teaspoons honey

½ avocado—peeled, pitted and diced, for garnish

2 to 3 tablespoons chopped cilantro, for garnish, optional

Warm 1 tablespoon of oil in a medium skillet over medium-high heat. Add the onion and jalapeño, season with a pinch of salt and cook, stirring occasionally, until tender and fragrant, 2 to 3 minutes. Add the garlic and continue to cook, stirring, 1 minute longer. Transfer the mixture to a bowl and let cool.

Place the tomatoes, cucumber, vinegar and basil into a blender; add the onion mixture. Cover and pulse to mix. Add half of the chopped peaches, ½ cup of vegetable juice and a couple of grinds of pepper and pulse until chopped and well mixed. Add more vegetable juice as needed, so that the mixture reaches a soupy consistency. Taste and season with salt and pepper. Add the honey, ½ teaspoon at a time, to balance the flavor, if needed (this will depend on how sweet your peaches and tomatoes were to begin with).

Transfer the soup to a bowl, cover and chill for at least 2 hours or up to 24 hours to let the flavors develop. Check the soup's consistency; thin with more vegetable juice if needed. Stir all but ½ cup of the remaining peaches into the soup. Taste and season with additional salt, pepper and honey, if desired. Ladle the gazpacho into bowls, drizzle with the remaining 2 tablespoons of oil, garnish with the reserved peaches, avocado and cilantro and serve.

Note: Even with half of the seeds from the jalapeño, this will be quite spicy. If you prefer less heat, remove all the seeds.

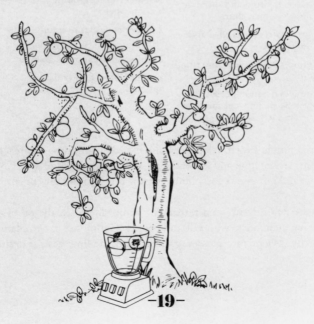

Halibut & Shrimp Ceviche

Ceviche is one of those things that doesn't seem as though it's going to work, but then it does, and the result is amazing. Peaches set this ceviche apart from others I've tried; the fruit's sweetness balances the salty fish and spicy jalapeño and makes the whole thing just scream "summer." Plus, the peaches add a burst of color that plays well with the pink in the shrimp and the green of the chile. This dish is perfect for hot weather because you never have to go near the stove; the acid from the citrus "cooks" the fish and quick-pickles the onion. Try serving it in small paper cups at a party.

½ small red onion, halved and very thinly sliced

1 large peach (or 2 small ones) —peeled, pitted and sliced or cut into ½-inch chunks

1 small jalapeño, seeded and thinly sliced

8 ounces halibut, cut into small chunks

8 ounces medium peeled and deveined shrimp, cut into 4 or 5 pieces each

⅓ cup fresh lime juice

¼ cup fresh lemon juice

Salt and freshly ground black pepper

2 tablespoons extra-virgin olive oil

2 tablespoons chopped cilantro

Zest of 1 lime, for garnish, optional

serves ·4·

Place the onion, peach, jalapeño, halibut and shrimp in a nonreactive bowl. Stir in the lime and lemon juices and a large pinch of salt. Cover the bowl and refrigerate for 1 hour, stirring every 15 minutes or so.

Drain the fish mixture and return to the bowl. Stir in the oil. Taste and season generously with salt and pepper. Gently stir in the cilantro. Spoon the ceviche into glasses, garnish with the lime zest, if desired, and serve.

Grilled Rack of Lamb with Peach Barbecue Sauce

Fatty meats and tangy fruit sauces are a classic combo, whether you go highbrow (*duck a l'orange*) or homestyle (ribs with barbecue sauce). This recipe is a little of both; it has the eat-with-your-hands informality of ribs and the dressiness of rack of lamb. Since the dish features universally loved peaches as the fruit, the whole thing is even more accessible and friendly. Go ahead, pick up the chops and gnaw away; I won't judge.

1 rack of lamb (1½ to 2 pounds)

Peach Barbecue Sauce (recipe on page 36)

Salt and freshly ground black pepper

serves
-4-

Remove the lamb from the refrigerator and bring to room temperature (about 20 minutes). Prepare a gas or charcoal grill with a very hot and a cooler side for both direct and indirect heat. Place 1 cup of barbecue sauce and a brush next to the grill (reserve the remaining sauce at room temperature).

Score the fat on the lamb with a sharp knife and season all over with salt and pepper. Grill the lamb over direct heat, fatty-side down, until well browned, about 6 minutes.

Turn the lamb and grill over direct heat until the meaty side is well browned on the bottom, about 3 minutes. Brush the lamb rack all over with sauce, turn and place, fatty side down, over indirect heat. Cover the grill and cook for 10 to 20 minutes, until an instant-read thermometer inserted in the center of the meat reads 130° for medium-rare. Transfer the lamb to a cutting board and let rest for 10 minutes.

Cut the rack into chops and serve, passing the reserved sauce at the table.

Pork al Pastor Tacos with Peach-Pineapple Salsa

Pork al pastor is a favorite dish in Mexico, adapted from the spit-roasted shawarma of Lebanese immigrants. Spiced lamb morphed into pork marinated in a paste made from chiles and vinegar and pita became corn tortillas, but the dish has retained its roots as a flavorful, messy street food perfect for late-night noshing. In my version, peaches mellow the acidity of and lend a bit of creaminess to al pastor's traditional pineapple and add brightness to the accompanying salsa.

For the pork:

1 ripe medium peach (about 5 ounces)—peeled, pitted and chopped

1 canned chipotle chile, plus 1 teaspoon adobo sauce

2 tablespoons extra-virgin olive oil, plus more for the grill

1 tablespoon cider vinegar

2 garlic cloves, minced (about 2 teaspoons)

1 tablespoon chile powder

1 teaspoon dried oregano

1 teaspoon cumin

1 tablespoon honey

Salt and freshly ground black pepper

One 1½- to 2-pound pork tenderloin, sliced ¾-inch thick

For the salsa:

12 ounces ripe peaches (about 2 to 3 medium), pitted and cut into small dice

4 ounces fresh pineapple, cut into small dice (scant 1 cup)

½ cup diced red onion

2 to 3 tablespoons lime juice

3 tablespoons chopped cilantro

Honey, optional

Kosher salt and freshly ground black pepper

For the tacos:

8 to 12 small corn or flour tortillas, for serving

Your favorite taco fixings

serves
·6·

Marinate the pork: In a blender or food processor, blend the peach, chipotle and adobo sauce, oil, vinegar, garlic, chile powder, oregano, cumin and honey until smooth. Taste and season with salt and pepper. Place the pork slices in a large Ziploc bag. Add the peach-chipotle marinade, seal the bag and shake to coat the meat with the sauce; refrigerate, turning the bag over occasionally, at least 2 hours or up to overnight.

Make the salsa: In a bowl, combine the peaches, pineapple, red onion and 2 tablespoons of lime juice. Fold in the cilantro. Season with salt and pepper. Taste and add more lime juice and/or honey to balance the flavor. Cover and refrigerate until ready to serve (this is best if it has a couple of hours to develop).

Prepare a hot gas or charcoal grill. Remove the pork slices from the marinade (discard excess marinade). Oil the grill grates and grill the pork, turning once, about 3 to 5 minutes a side. Transfer the pork to a plate, cover with foil and let rest for 10 minutes. Cut the pork into cubes. Serve with salsa, tortillas and any other taco fixings you like.

Chipotle Turkey Meatloaf with Peach Glaze

Here's a twist on meatloaf, with oats as a binder and turkey instead of beef. A generous slather of peach glaze stands in for the traditional ketchup and balances the spiciness of the meat mixture. For the best flavor, use the fattiest turkey you can get. Needless to say, leftovers make great sandwiches the next day; try them on sourdough bread.

For the meatloaf:

2 canned chipotle chiles, seeded, plus 1 tablespoon adobo sauce

1 tablespoon cider vinegar

1 tablespoon honey

2 large eggs

1 tablespoon Worcestershire sauce

1 tablespoon tomato paste

1 garlic clove, crushed

½ teaspoon kosher salt

½ teaspoon freshly ground black pepper

½ small onion, finely minced

1 pound ground turkey (not 99 percent lean)

¾ cup rolled oats (not instant)

For the glaze:

½ cup Peach Preserves (recipe on page 39, or use store-bought)

1 tablespoon extra-virgin olive oil

2 teaspoons soy sauce

1 teaspoon Dijon mustard

1 teaspoon cider vinegar

½ teaspoon honey

serves
•6•

Make the meatloaf: Preheat the oven to 350° and oil a 9-by-5-inch loaf pan. In a food processor, pulse the chiles and adobo sauce, vinegar, honey, eggs, Worcestershire, tomato paste, garlic, salt and pepper until smooth. Transfer to a large bowl and add the onion, turkey and oats.

Mix gently but thoroughly with your hands. Lightly pack the mixture into the loaf pan. Bake for 30 minutes.

While the meatloaf is baking, make the glaze: Combine the preserves, oil, soy sauce, mustard, vinegar and honey in a blender; blend until smooth. *(Note: This makes a lot of glaze. If you prefer less, just use half, and either serve the remainder on the side or cover and freeze for a future meatloaf.)*

Carefully spread the glaze on top of the meatloaf and bake for 20 to 25 minutes longer (an instant-read thermometer inserted into the center should read 160°). Let the meatloaf stand for 5 to 10 minutes before slicing and serving.

Peach & Heirloom Tomato Galette

Galettes are such a delightful cheat. You get all of the goodness of a pie or tart without having to press the dough into a pan or crimp decorative edges. Pile some stuff onto a puff pastry sheet and bake—and the more rustic it looks, the better. I didn't peel the peach here partially in the spirit of rusticness, and partly because the unpeeled fruit plays well with the tomatoes, which are also unpeeled. The more varied the shapes and colors of the tomatoes you use, the better. Toss a salad while the galette bakes.

1 sheet frozen puff pastry, thawed

¼ cup prepared olive tapenade

10 to 12 ounces ripe heirloom tomatoes

1 medium peach, pitted and cut into thin wedges

1 ounce soft goat cheese, crumbled

Freshly cracked black pepper

Extra-virgin olive oil, for drizzling

Baby basil leaves, for garnish

serves
4 to 6

Place a rack in center of the oven and preheat to 400°. Line a large baking sheet with parchment paper.

Unroll the pastry onto the parchment paper. Prick the center of the dough all over with a fork, leaving a 1-inch unpricked border around the edges. Spread the tapenade in the center of the dough. Slice the tomatoes into wedges or halves (depending on their size) and arrange the tomatoes and peach wedges over the tapenade. You can arrange the fruit in a pattern or haphazardly depending on which style you prefer. Sprinkle the goat cheese over the fruit, season with pepper and drizzle with 2 tablespoons of oil.

Bake the galette until the pastry has puffed up around the edges and is golden and crisp, about 30 minutes. Drizzle with additional oil and season with additional pepper, if desired. Just before serving, sprinkle the baby basil leaves over the galette (if you have only larger basil leaves, roughly chop or slice them into ribbons before sprinkling over the galette). Serve warm.

Green Goddess Chicken Salad with Peaches

Many years ago, a chef I worked for told me, "You can make kumquat soufflé all you want, but what makes people smile is milk and cookies. Just make it the best damn milk and cookies they ever had." In other words, start with classic favorites and elevate them. Take chicken salad: The simple act of using peaches —peaches!—in place of the typical apples or grapes feels rebellious but familiar. Instead of mixing it up with plain old mayo, use a creamy, herby green goddess dressing, and suddenly it's not your mama's chicken salad.

1 oil-packed anchovy fillet

1 teaspoon oil from anchovies

1 scallion, chopped

1 small garlic clove, minced

¼ cup parsley leaves

2 tablespoons chopped chives

2 tablespoons tarragon leaves

2 tablespoons fresh lemon juice

½ cup sour cream

¼ cup mayonnaise

Salt and freshly ground black pepper

One 2- to 3-pound rotisserie chicken, skin and bones discarded, meat cut or torn into bite-size pieces (about 4 cups)

1 large or 2 small peaches (about 8 ounces), pitted and chopped

1 medium fennel bulb, cored and cut into ¼-inch dice

2 ribs celery, halved lengthwise and sliced ¼-inch thick

Bibb lettuce leaves

2 tablespoons roasted, salted sunflower seeds

serves 4 to 6

Make the dressing: Place the anchovy fillet in a food processor or blender. Place the anchovy oil in a small skillet with the scallion and garlic. Turn the heat to medium and cook until the mixture begins to sizzle, about 1 minute. Stir and cook for 30 seconds longer (don't let the onion and garlic brown; this is just to tame the raw flavors). Scrape the mixture into the food processor with the anchovy and add the parsley, chives, tarragon and lemon juice. Process until the ingredients are chopped. Add the sour cream and mayonnaise and process until well-combined and bright green. Taste and season with salt and pepper, and an additional teaspoon or two of lemon juice, if desired. Leftover dressing can be refrigerated for up to 3 days.

In a large bowl, toss 3 cups of chicken (save any remaining meat for another use) with the peaches, fennel and celery. Add half the dressing and use your fingers to gently toss until coated. Add more dressing as needed until the mixture is well coated. (You may have extra dressing.)

Tear the lettuce leaves and divide among plates. Spoon some of the chicken salad onto the lettuce on each plate, sprinkle with sunflower seeds and serve. (Alternatively, you may cover and refrigerate the salad to serve later; if so, keep the extra dressing to mix in just before serving, if desired.)

Grilled Peach Pasta Salad with Burrata & Basil Vinaigrette

This is a twist on Caprese, the ubiquitous tomato-basil-mozzarella salad. Take this version to a party, don't tell anyone what's in it and watch their faces as they discover the many layers of flavor here. Peaches are similar to tomatoes in that they're sweet and slightly acidic, they're colorful and they go well with cheese—all elements that make them a great twist on the classic. Grilling the peaches adds a smoky element, which is intensified with a sprinkle of chile powder. Make sure when you're cutting up the burrata that 1) you don't eat it all and 2) you capture the liquid inside. When you mix the cheese in with the dressing and the chile-dusted peaches, it's magic. For the record, you can serve the chile-spiked grilled peaches on their own for dessert, with a drizzle of honey or alongside some vanilla ice cream.

For the dressing:

1 garlic clove, minced (about 1 teaspoon)

½ cup extra-virgin olive oil, divided

1¼ cups tightly packed fresh basil leaves

⅓ cup white balsamic vinegar

Salt and freshly ground black pepper

1 to 2 teaspoons honey, optional

For the salad:

4 medium firm-ripe peaches (about 1¼ pounds), halved and pitted

2 tablespoons extra-virgin olive oil

¼ teaspoon chile powder

Salt and freshly ground black pepper

One 16-ounce box short pasta (such as penne)

12 ounces burrata, drained and roughly chopped

⅓ cup toasted sliced almonds, optional

serves
6 to 8

Prepare a gas or charcoal grill for indirect grilling with medium-hot and cooler sides.

Make the dressing: Place the garlic in a small skillet and add 1 tablespoon of oil. Turn the heat to medium-low and wait just until the oil and garlic mixture begins to sizzle. Scrape the mixture into a blender. Add the remaining oil, basil and vinegar and blend until smooth. Taste and season with salt and pepper. Taste again and blend in the honey, if desired.

Brush the cut sides of the peaches with oil. Sprinkle lightly with salt and season with chile powder. Grill, cut sides down, over direct heat with the grill covered until grill marks appear on the fruit, about 3 minutes. Brush the tops of the peaches with oil, turn and place over the cool side of the grill. Cover and grill until the peaches are tender, 10 to 15 minutes. Remove the peaches from the grill, let cool, then coarsely chop.

Bring a pot of salted water to a boil. Add the pasta, stir and cook until al dente. Drain the pasta and run briefly under cold water to stop it from cooking. Drain well. Transfer the pasta to a large bowl. Add the grilled peaches and burrata (along with any liquid from inside the burrata pieces) and toss. Add the dressing and toss well. Season with additional salt and pepper, sprinkle with almonds, if desired, and serve.

Peach Upside-Down Cake

Take a tarte Tatin, mate it with a buttery cake and the resulting love child is this fancy-looking but simple dessert. The strong butter flavor and a little hint of ginger are a delicious setting for the slightly boozy, very brown sugary sautéed peaches. Except for a moment when you have to be a bit careful spreading the batter over the cooked peaches, this cake is ridiculously simple to make, but the result is very pretty. I think the cake tastes best warm, but it's good the next day, too. Don't forget the ice cream or freshly whipped cream.

12 tablespoons (1½ sticks) unsalted butter, at room temperature, divided, plus more for the pan

1¼ cups all-purpose flour

1 teaspoon ground ginger

½ teaspoon baking powder

¼ teaspoon baking soda

¼ teaspoon plus a pinch salt

¾ cup packed dark brown sugar

2 teaspoons vanilla extract, divided

3 tablespoons bourbon

2 to 3 medium-ripe peaches (8 to 12 ounces)—peeled, pitted and sliced

¾ cup granulated sugar

2 large eggs, at room temperature

½ cup buttermilk, at room temperature

Ice cream or whipped cream, for serving

serves
8

Place a rack in the center of the oven and preheat to 350°. Butter a 9-inch-round cake pan. In a bowl, combine the flour, ginger, baking powder, baking soda and salt; whisk until well mixed and set aside.

Cut 4 tablespoons of butter into slices and place in a large skillet. Add the brown sugar, 1 teaspoon of vanilla, bourbon and a pinch of salt and cook over medium-low heat, stirring occasionally, until the butter has melted and the mixture is well combined. Add the peach slices and cook, gently stirring occasionally, until they begin to soften and their liquid thickens, 7 to 9 minutes.

Using a slotted spoon or tongs, remove the peach slices and arrange them in circles in the bottom of the cake pan, beginning on the outside and moving into the middle of the pan, overlapping if necessary (you may not use all of the slices; save any extras for snacking or another use). Pour the remaining juices from the skillet over the peaches, taking care not to move them.

In a separate bowl, using an electric mixer, beat the remaining 8 tablespoons of butter with the granulated sugar at medium-high speed until light and fluffy, 2 to 3 minutes. Add the eggs, one at a time, beating well after each addition. Scrape down the side of the bowl. Using a wooden spoon or sturdy spatula, stir in half of the flour mixture, followed by the buttermilk and remaining teaspoon of vanilla, then the remaining flour mixture, stirring until just combined.

Using an offset spatula, gently spread the batter over the peaches, taking care not to move them too much. Bake for 30 to 40 minutes, until the cake is golden and bounces back when lightly pressed in the center. Let the cake cool in the pan on a wire rack for 5 minutes. Run a knife along the outer edge of the pan and invert the cake onto a serving dish. If any peach slices are stuck in the baking pan, carefully place them on top of the cake. Serve warm or at room temperature with ice cream or whipped cream.

Tropical Fruit Crisp

With all the dietary restrictions out there these days, something as simple as having friends over for dinner can be a real challenge. Good news: This crisp is vegan, thanks to coconut oil (instead of butter) in the topping. But the medley of tropical fruits delivers enough richness and flavor to keep even your most omnivorous guests happy. The peach doesn't technically qualify as a "tropical" fruit the way pineapple and mango do, but it plays diplomat here, mellowing the sharpness of the pineapple and taming the aggressive sweetness of the mango. Serve the crisp warm, with vanilla ice cream (vegan or otherwise) or coconut sorbet.

For the topping:

5 tablespoons virgin coconut oil, melted and cooled, plus more for the pan

1 cup rolled oats (not instant)

¾ cup all-purpose flour

½ cup packed dark brown sugar

2 teaspoons ground ginger

¼ teaspoon kosher salt

¼ cup finely chopped roasted, lightly salted macadamia nuts (1 ounce)

¼ cup unsweetened coconut flakes

For the filling:

1½ pounds firm, ripe peaches (about 5 medium)—peeled, pitted and chopped (about 4 cups)

1¼ cups chopped mango (about 1 mango)

1 cup chopped pineapple (about 5 ounces)

½ cup granulated sugar

⅓ cup all-purpose flour

1 tablespoon light rum

⅛ teaspoon salt

serves 6 to 8

Preheat the oven to 350°. Lightly grease a 9-inch pie plate with coconut oil. Line a large, rimmed baking sheet with foil.

Make the topping: In a bowl, combine the oats, flour, brown sugar, ginger and salt. Stir in the 5 tablespoons of coconut oil until all the dry ingredients are moistened and the mixture is crumbly. Toss in the nuts and coconut. Refrigerate while you make the filling.

Make the filling: In a bowl, toss the peaches, mango and pineapple with the granulated sugar, flour, light rum and salt. Let stand for 5 minutes. Transfer the fruit to the prepared pie plate. Sprinkle the topping evenly over the filling, place the dish on the baking sheet and bake until the fruit bubbles and the topping is golden, 35 to 40 minutes. Let cool on a wire rack. Serve warm or at room temperature.

Peach-Campari Sorbet

Not everyone loves Campari: Its distinctly herby, bitter taste can take some getting used to (this is a skill I have mastered). This sorbet includes just a bit—too much and it won't freeze properly— and the intense sweetness of the peaches keeps that bitterness in check. This sorbet is distinctly grown-up and a really good palate cleanser after a flavorful or rich meal.

---

3 pounds peaches (about 10 medium)—peeled, pitted and chopped

1 tablespoon freshly squeezed orange juice

½ cup plus 2 tablespoons sugar

¼ cup Campari

¼ teaspoon kosher salt

In a blender, blend the peaches, orange juice, sugar, Campari and salt until smooth. Cover and chill in the refrigerator until very cold, at least 3 hours.

Scrape the puree into an ice cream maker and churn according to the manufacturer's instructions. Transfer to an airtight freezer-safe container, cover and freeze until firm, at least 4 hours, before serving.

Peach Pie
with Brown-Butter Custard

I sometimes hear people say, "Oh, I don't like pie, I'm a cake person," or vice versa. To me this is crazy. Personally, I like dessert in just about any form. (Then again, if you're a "cake person," then more pie for me!) I love custard pies, in part because they don't require a top crust—I'm all about the filling. A custardy peach pie is a particular favorite of mine, because peaches and cream is such a perfect, poetic combination. The brown butter gives this pie a nutty edge, while the brown sugar contributes a caramel note.

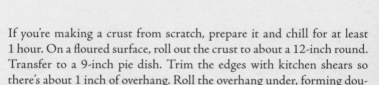

One 9-inch pie crust, frozen (store-bought or see recipe in *Note*)

4 tablespoons unsalted butter, cut into pieces

¾ cup sour cream

¾ cup packed dark brown sugar

4 large egg yolks

¼ cup all-purpose flour

1 teaspoon vanilla extract

¼ teaspoon kosher salt

1¼ pounds peaches (about 4 medium)—peeled, pitted and cut into thick slices or thin wedges

makes one **9** IN. *pie*

If you're making a crust from scratch, prepare it and chill for at least 1 hour. On a floured surface, roll out the crust to about a 12-inch round. Transfer to a 9-inch pie dish. Trim the edges with kitchen shears so there's about 1 inch of overhang. Roll the overhang under, forming double-thick edges, and crimp. Place the pie shell in the freezer.

Make the filling: Place the butter in a medium skillet or small saucepan and melt over medium heat, stirring occasionally with a heatproof spatula. Cook, adjusting the temperature as needed, until the butter simmers and foams. Watch carefully to prevent it from burning. Continue to simmer, stirring often, until the butter turns golden brown and smells nutty, 3 to 5 minutes. Remove the pan from the heat and immediately transfer the butter to a small bowl to cool.

Place a foil-lined baking sheet on the center rack in the oven and preheat to 425°. In a medium bowl, whisk the sour cream, brown sugar, egg yolks, flour, vanilla and salt until well combined. When the butter has cooled so that it's barely warm to the touch, whisk it into the sour cream mixture.

Pat the peach slices dry with a paper towel. Remove the crust from the freezer and arrange the peach slices in the crust. Gently pour the sour cream mixture over the peaches. Lift the pan and lightly drop the pie on the counter to pop any air bubbles.

Place the pie on the preheated baking sheet and bake for 35 to 40 minutes, rotating the sheet halfway through cooking, until the custard is puffed and lightly browned and no longer jiggles when the pie is lightly shaken. (Watch the pie carefully; if the crust browns too quickly, add a foil tent on top during the remainder of the baking time.) Let the pie cool on a rack for 2 hours (it will settle), then cover loosely with foil and refrigerate until cold, at least 3 hours. Serve cold.

Note: If you like to make your own pie crust (as I do), here's a recipe. I make enough for two crusts and then freeze one for later. (I do a little happy dance whenever I'm about to make pie and there's already a crust in the freezer.) Be sure all of your ingredients are cold. Cut 16 table-spoons (2 sticks) cold, unsalted butter into small pieces, then wrap in plastic wrap and freeze. In a food processor, pulse together 2½ cups of all-purpose flour and ¾ teaspoon of salt. Separate the butter pieces as you drop them into the processor, then pulse until the mixture looks like coarse meal. Add 2 tablespoons of ice-cold vodka and 3 tablespoons of ice-cold water and pulse just until the dough forms clumps. (If the dough is too dry, add more water 1 teaspoon at a time and pulse, but don't let the mixture get wet and try not to overwork it.) Gather the dough into a ball, divide in half, form into discs and wrap separately in plastic wrap. Refrigerate one disc for at least 1 hour and up to a day; place the other in a freezer bag and freeze for another use (cue happy dance). You can replace half of the butter with vegetable shortening if you like.

Peach Barbecue Sauce

These days, there are endless bottled barbecue sauce options, but I think the homemade stuff is usually a thousand times better, and making it requires less effort than you might think. (Same with granola, but I digress.) Peaches lend a more complex form of sweetness than the plain brown sugar or molasses that is typical in barbecue sauce, and bacon adds a little smokiness and depth. This sauce is perfect for lamb (see recipe on page 21), pork loin or chicken. If you have peaches that are a little bruised or overripe, toss them in—blemishes won't matter here.

---

2 slices uncured bacon, chopped

½ cup finely chopped sweet onion (such as Vidalia; about ⅓ small onion)

1 medium jalapeño, seeded and minced (about 3 tablespoons)

1 pound ripe peaches—peeled, pitted and chopped

¼ cup cider vinegar

¼ cup bourbon

2 tablespoons honey

2 tablespoons Dijon mustard

1 tablespoon tomato paste

1 tablespoon packed brown sugar

½ teaspoon chile powder

¼ teaspoon dry mustard

¼ teaspoon kosher salt

¼ teaspoon freshly ground black pepper

makes 1¾ cups

In a medium saucepan, cook the bacon over medium heat, stirring, until the bacon is crisp and the fat has been rendered, about 5 minutes. Using a slotted spoon, transfer the bacon to a paper-towel-lined plate. (Cover and refrigerate for another use.) Add the onion and jalapeño to the skillet with the bacon fat and cook, stirring, until just tender, about 5 minutes. Add the peaches and continue to cook until they're slightly softened, about 5 minutes longer.

Stir in the vinegar, bourbon, honey, mustard, tomato paste, brown sugar, chile powder and dry mustard. Reduce the heat to medium-low and simmer, stirring occasionally, until the peaches are very tender, 20 to 30 minutes. Remove the pan from the heat and let cool slightly. Transfer the mixture to a blender and blend until smooth (take care when blending hot liquids). Taste and season with salt and pepper. Use right away, or cover and refrigerate for up to 7 days.

Bourbon Peach Sauce

I love to corrupt sweet, innocent peaches with something wicked —in this case, bourbon. You can pair this simple sauce with lots of things: pound cake, waffles, pancakes, French toast. My favorite use for it is as a topping on really high-quality vanilla ice cream. I like the consistency as it is, but you can also puree the sauce, which produces a texture that's more like applesauce. But make no mistake: This boozy sauce is strictly for grown-ups.

½ cup sugar

⅓ cup bourbon

Generous pinch of salt

1½ pounds ripe peaches (about 5 medium)—peeled, pitted and sliced

makes **2** cups

In a large saucepan, combine the sugar, bourbon and salt. Add the peaches and bring to a boil over medium-high heat, stirring until the sugar has dissolved. Reduce the heat to medium-low and cook at a brisk simmer, stirring often, until thickened, about 15 minutes. Let cool slightly and serve warm or cool completely, transfer to a jar, cover and refrigerate for up to a month.

Peach-Onion Relish

Peaches and sweet onions go together beautifully, and they're a popular combo in the American South. I've sampled plenty of relishes that marry these two ingredients, and there's often lots of spice in there, too: cloves, cinnamon, sometimes mustard seed. This version lets the peaches and onions speak for themselves, with just a bit of ginger for heat. It's a great accompaniment for grilled steak, but would be equally at home on a hot dog.

2½ cups cider vinegar

1 cup sugar

1 tablespoon kosher salt

½ teaspoon crushed red pepper flakes

One 2-inch piece fresh ginger, peeled and minced (about 2 tablespoons)

Freshly ground black pepper

1 pound firm peaches—peeled, pitted and thinly sliced

½ medium sweet onion (such as Vidalia), very thinly sliced

In a saucepan, combine the vinegar, 1 cup of water, sugar, salt, red pepper flakes and ginger. Add a few grinds of freshly ground black pepper. Bring to a simmer over medium heat, stirring to dissolve the sugar and salt, about 5 minutes. Add the peaches and onion to the saucepan; stir and bring to a boil over medium-high heat. Reduce the heat to medium-low, cover and simmer until the peaches and onion are tender, 5 to 10 minutes.

Let cool, then use a slotted spoon to transfer the peaches, onion and ginger to a clean 4-cup canning jar. Add enough pickling liquid to cover the solids. Cover the jar and refrigerate for at least 24 hours before using. The relish will keep, covered and refrigerated, for up to 3 weeks.

Note: You may end up with a lot of liquid when the relish is done. Don't worry; simply drain off most of it before storing the relish.

Peach Preserves

The first time I made jam, I was a very young cook working at a bed-and-breakfast in Venice, California. The manager came in with a flat of strawberries, gave me a stern look, said, "Make jam," and left. Thanks to *The Joy of Cooking*, it wasn't a disaster, and I've loved it ever since. A few years ago, I read an article in *The New York Times* about French jam maker Christine Ferber, who macerates the fruit overnight, cooks the resulting syrup first and then returns the fruit to the cooked syrup. I've adopted her method, which results in jam that just screams fruit. This is especially important with peach preserves. I find the jarred stuff is sometimes just so sweet but lacking any of the subtlety or fragrance of peaches. Using this method, the fruit itself isn't cooked as much, so it retains its essential peachiness.

1½ pounds ripe peaches (about 5 medium)—peeled, pitted and chopped

¾ cup sugar

Juice of ½ lemon (about 2 tablespoons)

Generous pinch of kosher salt

makes 1½ cups

Combine the peaches, sugar, lemon juice and salt in a large bowl. Cover and refrigerate for at least 8 hours or overnight.

Place a fine-mesh sieve over a large saucepan. Pour the peach mixture into the sieve and let the fruit's juices collect in the pan. Reserve the solids, place the pan over medium heat and bring to a boil. Boil, stirring often, until the liquid is syrupy and reduced by half, about 8 minutes. Add the peach mixture to the pan and bring back to a boil. Cook, stirring occasionally, until the peaches are very soft, 15 to 20 minutes. Crush the peaches with the back of a wooden spoon as they cook (for a smoother preserve, use an immersion blender). Transfer the preserves to a large bowl to cool.

Spoon the peach preserves into a pint-size jar with a tight-fitting lid and refrigerate. The preserves will keep, covered and refrigerated, for up to 3 weeks. Or seal the preserves in sterilized jars using the boiling water method and store at room temperature.

Peach Snapper

All hail Fernand Petiot, the bartender at the King Cole Bar at the St. Regis Hotel in New York City, who, in 1934, introduced a spicy tomato cocktail with vodka that he called the Bloody Mary. That name proved too provocative for St. Regis patrons, so it was renamed the Red Snapper. No matter what you call it, it's a jewel, a perfect recipe. And, like other classic dishes, it's prime for experimentation. This version replaces tomato juice with sunny peaches and peach juice. The result softens the Bloody Mary from its savory stance, making it just as appropriate for the beach as the bar.

2 very ripe peaches—peeled, pitted and roughly chopped

One 32-ounce bottle peach nectar or juice (such as R.W. Knudsen), divided

Juice of 1 lime

3 tablespoons Worcestershire sauce

2 to 5 dashes hot sauce

1 tablespoon freshly ground black pepper

1 tablespoon cayenne

1½ teaspoons celery salt

Vodka

In a blender, combine the peaches with 1 cup of peach nectar; blend until smooth. Add the remaining peach nectar, lime juice, Worcestershire sauce, hot sauce (start with 2 dashes), pepper, cayenne and celery salt. Blend until well combined. Taste and season with additional hot sauce, if desired. Transfer the mixture to a container, cover and refrigerate for 8 hours.

To serve, fill highball glasses with ice. Add 1 of ounce vodka and 8 to 10 ounces of the Peach Snapper mix to each glass, stir and serve.

Mayahuel's Revenge

Several years ago at Manhattan's Craftbar restaurant, I had an amazing cocktail made with tequila, cucumber and jalapeño, garnished with mint. It was a revelation: spicy, vegetal and refreshing—and not overly sweet, as many fancy drinks are. When thinking about peach cocktails for this book, I immediately remembered the flavors of that drink. I kept the cucumber and jalapeño, swapped smoky mezcal for the tequila and added peach juice, the sweetness of which balances everything out. I named it for the Mexican goddess of fertility. (Google her; it's a pretty wild story.)

For the spicy mezcal:

1 cup mezcal

½ to 1 small jalapeño, halved and seeded

For the cucumber simple syrup:

1 cup sugar

1 cup coarsely grated English cucumber

For the cocktail:

2 ounces peach juice (such as R.W. Knudsen Peach Nectar)

Club soda

Peach slices, for garnish

Lime wedges, for garnish

Make the spicy mezcal: Combine the mezcal and jalapeño in a glass jar. Cover and let infuse at room temperature for about 1 hour. Strain the mezcal through a fine-mesh sieve, discard the solids and transfer the mezcal to a lidded container or bottle. Refrigerate until ready to use.

Make the simple syrup: In a saucepan, bring the sugar and 1 cup of water to a boil over medium-high heat, stirring to dissolve the sugar.

Remove the pan from the heat, stir in the cucumber, cover and let steep for 30 minutes. Strain the mixture through a fine-mesh sieve, pressing down on the solids to extract as much liquid as possible. Discard the solids, cover the simple syrup and refrigerate until ready to use.

Make the cocktail: Fill a mixing glass with ice. Add 1 to 1½ ounces of spicy mezcal, 1 ounce of cucumber simple syrup and the peach juice. Stir well, then strain into an ice-filled rocks glass. Fill to the rim with club soda. Garnish the glass with a peach slice and lime wedge and serve. (The remaining mezcal and simple syrup can be refrigerated in airtight containers for up to 1 month.)

Thank You!

First off, a big thanks to Nick and Kaitlyn for this fantastic opportunity to join the esteemed Short Stack family.

Thanks to my new friends in New Orleans, for their support and their palates. Huge thanks to my amazing colleagues and friends who so graciously tested recipes: Maryann Pomeranz, Lori Powell, Charles Pierce, Paul Grimes, Cecily McAndrews and Andrea Strong.

To Clare McHugh, the best boss in the world and a truly great friend, for always supporting and encouraging me. To my mother, the most original and most loving person I know, who still makes the best brisket and hello dollies I've ever tasted. Thanks for being my cheerleader, always. To Dylan, my sunshine, thank you for being patient with me and for tasting some new things.

Last but certainly not least, to Mark, thank you for... everything.

—*Beth Lipton*

Share your Short Stack cooking experiences with us
(or just keep in touch) via:

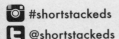

#shortstackeds   facebook.com/shortstackeditions
@shortstackeds   hello@shortstackeditions.com

Colophon

This edition of Short Stack was printed by Circle Press in New York City on Neenah Astrobrights Pulsar Pink (interior) and Neenah Oxford White (cover) paper. The main text of the book is set in Futura and Jensen Pro, and the headlines are set in Lobster.

Sewn by: W.E

Available now at
ShortStackEditions.com: